SYMBOL ODYSSEY:

GUIDEBOOK TO THE 108 UNCOMPROMISING PRINCIPLES OF WISDOM AND TRUTH

AUTHORS
BARBARA DAVIS-THOMPSON, LCSW

JOSHUA J. MARK, MA

Copyright

Zenzar Design, LLC
Ordinary Truth, Extraordinarily Lived.

Symbol Odyssey: Guidebook to the 108 Uncompromising Principles of Wisdom and Truth

Writings by Barbara Davis-Thompson, LCSW and Joshua Mark, M.A. © Zenzar Design, LLC

Symbol illustrations and cover art by Kevin Yong-Moon Lee. © Zenzar Design, LLC

All rights reserved © 2017. No part of this publication maybe reproduced, distributed, or transmitted in any form or by any means, or stored in a database or retrieval system, without the prior written permission of the creators of this book.

Zenzar, Design, LLC
15 Stuyvesant Oval, 8F
New York, NY 10009
USA

Visit our web site at www.znzr.co.

ISBN-13: 978-0692944431
ISBN-10: 069294435

DEDICATION

For Parnell, who so many years ago reached out to a neglected child and showed her there were safe people who did care. My heart is so grateful that I have met you once again in this life time.

CONTENTS

1. Dedication ii
2. Preface iv
3. How to use Symbol Odyssey: Guidebook to the 108 Uncompromising Principles of Wisdom and Truth v
4. Symbols 01
5. Blessing 109
6. Themes 110
7. Contributors 117
8. Special Acknowledgement 119
9. Resources 120

PREFACE

Life took me by surprise when it began to speak to me through intuitive dreams and meditative visions, all of which came to form in the Symbol Lamp™ landscaped with symbols and images embodying 108 universal laws of wisdom and truth. The Symbol Lamp™ was created to be a beacon of truth, an Aladdin's lamp compass to evolved living. From my dream envisioned lamp this book evolved.

You are invited to explore the transformational energies of Symbol Odyssey: Guidebook to the 108 Uncompromising Principles of Truth and the Symbol Lamp™. These tools were created to bring ordinary truth to expanded awareness so it can be put to extraordinary use in support of personal growth, expanded consciousness, and the healing of our planet and all that exists on it.

Symbol Odyssey: Guidebook to the 108 Uncompromising Principles of Wisdom and Truth is an enrichment of the Symbol Lamp booklet, expanding upon the list of 108 universal laws found at www.twoworldswisdom.org. The book defines each universal principle and offers augmented information about each symbol and image as it relates to each principle. Every image and symbol was exclusively chosen or designed to lucidly and telepathically communicate to your conscious and subconscious minds.

- Barbara Davis-Thompson, 2017

How to use *Symbol Odyssey: Guidebook to the 108 Uncompromising Principles of Wisdom and Truth*

A book in a look! This phrase speak volumes about the massive amount of information that symbols and images embody; symbols are, after all, the earliest and most concise of all forms of communication. This symbol and image-filled book is meant to be a gateway of inspiration that can set in motion an extraordinary spiritual odyssey. It is hoped that the carefully chosen symbols and images will exert a mystical influence on your life.

There is no one way to use the book to access your most evolved intuitive intelligence. Just know that embedded in the universal images and symbols within the book is a flowing stream of vital energy that is intended to reformat extraordinary and enlightened responses to your life.

Believe that a transformation of consciousness will, in time, happen and eventually show up on the physical realm as you live the principles of universal wisdom and truth that are re-patterning to become automatic positive responses.

As you commit to living the truths and wisdoms you've chosen, you are invited to do a check-in at the end of each day, week, or month. Reflect on what you are doing to embrace and embody the principles. Recall how you are putting more illuminated patterns of behavior and thought into action. Ask yourself, "What other ways can I put into practice living the universal law(s) I have chosen to exemplify?"

You can also journal, writing about how engaging with the symbols and images in *Symbol Odyssey: Guidebook to the 108 Uncompromising Principles of Wisdom and Truth* is affecting you. Create a travelogue detailing the expansions and/or contractions at each level of awareness for each universal law you have chosen to spotlight. Always keep in mind and trust that the symbols and images are inspiring your life without you realizing it, that they are unfolding what has heretofore been outside your ordinary awareness.

Perhaps your path to a deepening relationship with the universal truths is through mediation or guided visualization. In such practices, you quiet the mind and hold a desire to make connection with the energy of the image or symbol you have selected as your focal point. Take three to five minutes to be in mindfulness, observing your inner world of feelings and thoughts as you energetically embrace the symbol or image. In time, your inner voice will instinctively guide you to evolved personal awareness and deeper spiritual insights.

It must be said that your journey with this book is no quick fix to catapult you painlessly to spiritual mastery - although at moments it could. However, it is more likely your trek will be a non-linear one with spiritual u-turns along the way, which Spanish mystic St. Juan de la Cruz explores in his poem 'The Dark Night' and his treatise 'Ascent of Mount Carmel'. Stanislav and Christina Grof later popularized in their writing such despairing times of spiritual collapse as the 'dark night of the soul'. Such moments of spiritual hopelessness are but a stage, or recurring stages, when the aspects of ordinary consciousness, the archaic distorted thought forms of humankind, flush to the surface to be purged. If and when such flashbacks erupt, revealing to you self-sabotaging patterns, shaming and painful memories, deeply despairing thoughts, and downright cruel past actions, understand this as part of the healing process. You can support yourself through such moments of archaic negativity by thanking these energies. Talk to these disparaging thoughts, flashbacks, and recriminations saying, "Thank you. You are reminding me of my ardent desire to become a person of impeccable character and to stop doing that which takes me out of my evolved self." Please stay the course and remember there is no common denominator in the journey of unfolding into your numinous self.

As much as possible, remember that *Symbol Odyssey: Guidebook to the 108 Uncompromising Principles of Wisdom and Truth* is a conduit to your subconscious mind bringing lower energies to higher expression, supporting evolution, love, and goodwill. As your relationship with the universal laws develops, trust that the visual slumber power of the symbols and imagery is activating your capacity to transcend personal will and is supporting you to become an evolved, enlightened personality acting as a channel for all that is above.

Enjoy your exploratory journey into the mysterious. Delight in feeling more spiritually alive as you embrace each symbol and image, letting them stimulate your imagination and motivate you to more joyfully and playfully relate each day in every present moment from truth and wisdom.

SYMBOLS

01

ABUNDANCE

Richness and plenitude are
present to achieve all you desire.

The Adinkra Nserewa reflects riches, agency,
and thriving. Action inspired by love is so
potent - it expands energy which can be directed
to create an abundance of anything you want.

02

ACCEPTANCE

It is necessary to accept what is
in order to change anything.

The Triangle Within a Circle is Alcoholic's
Anonymous's logo; it is embellished with
the Roman Numeral I inside the Triangle
which represents AA's 1st step of acceptance,
ever-reminding that only with acceptance
of what is can there be recovery/change.
"Accept what is, let go of what was, and have
faith in what will be." ~Author Unknown

03

ACCOUNTABILITY
To whom much is given,
much is required.

책임

The Korean writing for accountability speaks to stepping up into psychological and spiritual self-mastery by being answerable for all that you think, say, do, and feel. "It is not only what we do, but also what we do not do, for which we are accountable."
~Moliere

04

ACTION

Energy follows thought; set your goals first
and then take steps to meet them.

The Rune Stone Raidho embodies how
nothing can be achieved
without taking action.
As Mahatma Ghandi said,
"Action expresses priorities."

05

AKASHA

Akasha is the cosmic matter in which you
live, breathe, and take action.

The Hebrew writing for Yahweh,
a name too holy to even pronounce, is the
the very infinite, inconceivable essence
permeating all of creation. The mind of
every being is a reflection of Universal
Consciousness and is of the same substance as it.
"Ye are Gods; you are all sons {and daughters}
of the most High." ~Psalms 82:6

06

ANALOGY

That which you seek to understand is often grasped in terms of what you already know.

The Borromean symbol of three interconnected circles in which no two are directly linked implies that comparisons of unlike things can reveal similarities. "Truth, like gold, is to be obtained not by its growth, but by washing away from it all that is not gold." ~Leo Tolstoy

07

AS ABOVE
As above, so below.

The Unicursal Hexagram incorporates
this wisdom of the ancients which affirms man is
the correlate of God on earth
as God is man's correlate in heaven. "... the
universe is the same as God, God is the same
as man, man is the same as the cell, the cell is the
same as the atom..and so on, ad infinitum."
~Hermes Trismegistus

08

ASCENSION

As you become more aware,
you rise up to higher realms.

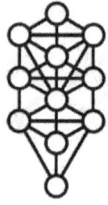

The Tree of Life image depicts the journey of
man's relationship to the cosmos
from human origin to apotheosis,
reaching the Light of Divine Understanding.
"In the kind of world we have today,
transformation of humanity might well be our
real hope for survival." ~Stanislav Grof

09

ATTACHMENT

Any connection takes time and
life-force energy from you.

The Embryo with Umbilical Cord symbolizes
your first physical connection which becomes
the driving force of later mental, social, and
emotional development that shapes lifelong
patterns of response. "A comfort zone is a
beautiful place but nothing ever grows there."
~Author Unknown

10

BALANCE

Whatever you put out into the universe will generate an equal return requiring restitution.

The Scales with the Karma Hindu symbol as fulcrum represents the law of correct proportions. Wayne Dyer writes, "How people treat you is their karma; how you react is yours." "...karma...continually {gives} the teachings that you need to open your heart." ~Pema Chodron

11

CHANGE

Any change, no matter how small, revises all.

The World Triad symbol depicts the
endlessly spiraling cycles of time with change
as a universal constant, revealing when change
occurs, at even the smallest levels,
it will have huge ripple effects.
"Never believe that a few, caring people can't
change the world. ...indeed, that's all who
ever have." ~Margaret Mead

12

COMPASSION
Empathy for others leads to deeper
connection with the others.

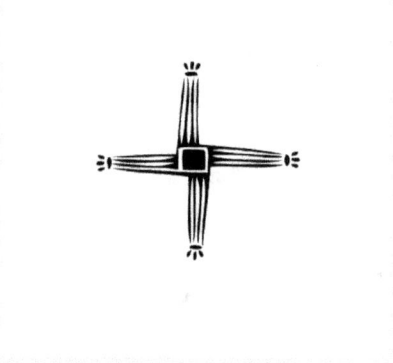

St. Brigid's Cross is a pre-Christian
symbol of the goddess Brigid,
synonymous with compassion.
The Dalai Lama says,
"Love and compassion are necessities, not luxuries.
Without them, humanity cannot survive."

13

CONNECTIVITY

That which is to you relates to all that is.

The Tibetan Buddhist Eternal Knot
symbolizes there is no beginning, no end,
just the movement of time and the endless
cycle of death and rebirth, a continual
journey acquiring perfect knowledge
of the complete oneness with everything.

14

CONSCIOUSNESS

Awareness is the underlying
measure of the cosmos.

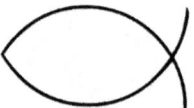

The Ichthys signifies the most basic grasp of
the universe consisting of varying levels of
consciousness, bespeaking the intersection
between heavenly and physical realms.
"Man's ethics must not end with man, but...extend
to the universe. He must regain the consciousness
of the great Chain of Life from which he
cannot be separated." ~Albert Schweitzer

15

CONTAGION

Whatever you connect with stays
with you even when you are apart.

The Romani Chakra represents heritage,
family, and cultural imprints, shaping
lifelong norms and roles. "I could see
the white man did not care for each other the
way our people did...They {took} from each
other if they could...some...had more of
everything than could {be used}, while crowds
had nothing...This could not be better than the
old ways of my people." ~Black Elk

16

CONTINUITY OF CONSCIOUSNESS

Awareness expands as the soul matures;
consciousness continues on higher levels.

The Ouroboros speaks of eternal return,
the descent of the spirit into the physical
world and its return over and over again until
pure consciousness is attained. The ouroboros
is one of the most ancient symbols in the
Spiritus Mundi symbolizing
transformation and rebirth.

17

CYCLES

To everything there is a season to be born,
to create, to release, and recede.

The Egyptian Goddess Hathor's crown
represents the endless moon rhythms that reflect
life cycles of birth to maturity to death back
to rebirth; with each stage of life,
the groundwork is laid for the next stage of life.
"I searched for God and found only myself.
I searched for myself and found only God." ~ Rumi

18

DECREE
That which created the All out-sources
to the ultimate limit.

The Zenzar Design Meditating Figure with Halo,
wand in one hand pointing to Source and
the other hand pointing down, indicates earthly
manifestation. Mankind is the Source's channel of
limitless creativity and the mirror reflecting it back.
"Don't only practice your art, but force your
way into its secrets. For it and knowledge can
raise men to the divine." ~Ludwig van Beethoven

19

DELEGATION

The cosmos responds to your wishes
as your soul advances in maturity.

The Seal of Shamash conveys Source assigned mankind stewardship of the heavens and earth to reflect back the wonders of creation, asking all souls to act collectively in sacred trust to wisely manage and preserve a sustainable earth community and to care for all of creation. "Humankind has not woven the web of life. We are but one thread within it. ...all things are bound. All things connect." ~Chief Seattle

20

DESIRE

When you act as if,
you become as you wish.

Adar's flame expresses you become
what you ardently envision.
This symbol is akin to the phrase 'fire in the belly'.
The greater the fire the more indomitable
you become, refusing to be defeated or overcome.
"Desire is the starting point of all achievement,
not a hope, not a wish, but a keen pulsating desire
which transcends everything." ~Napoleon Hill

21

DETACHMENT

When you let go of the need for results, your
range of influence increases exponentially.

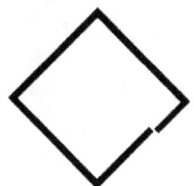

The Zenzar Design symbol conveys an impersonal
state of awareness. Buddha believed, "Suffering
is universal. The origin of suffering is attachment.
The cessation of suffering is attainable.
The Path to the cessation of suffering is
detachment." An unknown source says,
"Do not be owned by what you own."

22

DISCIPLINE

Self-discipline is the cornerstone of true choice.

The Adinkra Akoko Nan symbol is
synonymous with discipline.
If there is an inability to say
"no" to self and others,
greater freedom is ultimately lost and
others must say your "no's" for you.
"When you say "yes" to others, make sure
you are not saying "no" to yourself."
~Paulo Coelho

23

DIVINE FLOW

Aligning the four squares of your being - body, mind, heart, and soul - you become boundless.

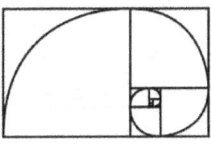

The Golden Mean image translates to
when all your energetic bodies are aligned,
divine flow is continuously experienced.
As the Kabbalah states, nothing exists
without receiving spiritual power
from divine flow.

24

DIVINE ONENESS

If the Source of all were a bonfire, everything that exists is a lick of flame reflective of Source and joining us all in all dimensions.

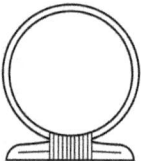

The Egyptian Shen symbolizes completeness and unity. It communicates that All is connected to All; I am you and you are me. Whatever affects one of us affects all of us. "The most important principle of divine philosophy is the oneness of the world of humanity, the unity of mankind, the bond conjoining East and West, the tie of love which blends human hearts." ~Abu'l-Baha

25

DYNAMIC BALANCE

Anything out of alignment with the Fountainhead
of life must be brought into relationship.

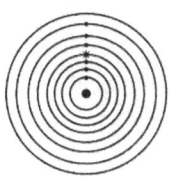

The Solar System image conveys the principle
of this concept of constant adjustment
within cycles and rhythms of energetic forces.
All that exists needs right relationship
on all planes of energy. "So divinely is our world
organized that every one of us, in our place and time,
is in balance with everything else."
~Johann Wolfgang von Goethe

26

ENERGY

After the demarcation of creation,
all is energy.

The Atom image reveals that energy is the building block of all matter. "If you want to find the secrets of the universe, think in terms of energy, frequency, and vibration. My brain is only a receiver; in the universe there is a core from which we obtain knowledge, strength, and inspiration. I have not penetrated into the secrets of this core, but I know it exists." ~Nikola Tesla

27

ESSENCE

Life is impersonal; it doesn't need for you to like what is - only for you to accept what is.

The Adinkra Gye Nyame embeds the principle that truth encompasses everything and functions impersonally as All thinking in every moment. Living from and in truth without ego distortions is mankind's sacred spiritual mission in bringing about perfected humanity.
"Everything has a spirit - honor that."
~Chief Arvol Looking Horse

28

EXPANDED CONSCIOUSNESS

Expanded awareness creates an ability to
live in a larger, unbounded world.

The Mayan symbol Ahau has as one of its
meanings ascension to the Mind of Light
which has no limits, no completion.
Souls are continuously progressing and ascending
at multitudinal dimensions of higher sentience.
"Imagine how the world would be if everyone was
taught to believe they were limitless and eternal."
~Unknown Author

29

EXPANDED CONTEXT

Everything is comprehensible yet never fully
known as the Source of All has no limits.

The Tao Golden Pathway symbol illustrates
how energy frequencies must be ever raised
in order to realize higher states of consciousness.
The journey of realization is an inconceivable,
illuminative process toward limitless boundlessness.
Zoom in on the magical, amazing, enraptured and
synchronous life moments and the cosmos will
keep giving them to you.

30

FEAR

Fear is an ego construct; the soul's highest wisdom knows there is only love.

The Hamsa is an ancient symbol used as protection against fear which when distorted builds ego defenses and faulty thoughts. Healthy understanding of fear is to let it inform when something isn't true or right, thus corrective action can be taken. "Your largest fear carries your greatest growth."
~Author Unknown

31

FORGIVENESS

If you cannot forgive, you enslave yourself
to the energy of blame.

The Dove is a universal image of
pardon and reconciliation.
Only the path of forgiveness can
pave the way for breakthrough.
"Never ruin an apology with an excuse."
~Benjamin Franklin

32

FREE WILL

The boundaries of the Life Force
Energy are your boundaries as well.

The Native American Eagle figure represents
individual freedom and endless creative power
within infinity. "The Creator..shrouding with
mystery His presence in every atom of creation...
has but one motive -...that men seek Him only
through free will." ~Paramahansa Yogananda

33

GIVING

Giving and receiving are two sides of the same coin;
to give is to receive and to receive is to give.

The Adinkra Woforo Dua Pa symbolizes
giving and receiving are one.
Isabel Allende writes,
"We only have what we give."
Mother Theresa is quoted as saying,
"It is not how much we give but
how much love we put into giving."

34

GOODWILL

Leave any person, place, thing,
or situation better than you found it.

The Eight Pointed Star design calls you to live
and respond with patience, understanding,
and kindness. In so doing, you create a mindset
that endeavors to, at all times in all ways, become
a center of expression for the Primal Will-to-Good.
"If the courage to endure everything with
goodwill is lacking, good will is crippled."
~Mahatma Gandhi

35

GRACE

Living from grace eases bad karma.

The Celtic Arwen symbolizes
the law of reciprocity and grace,
which allows staying respectful, even loving,
when dealing with people at their
most unlovable. Anne Lamott writes,
"I do not understand the mystery of grace -
only that it meets us where we are but
does not leave us where it found us."

36

GRATITUDE

Increased gratitude results in greater joy
at what you have been given.

The Zenzar Design Carnation image depicts
appreciation, especially to Gaia, the sustainer of
all life, and to womankind, who gestate life.
"Be thankful for what you have;
you'll end up having more.
If you concentrate on what you don't have,
you will never, ever have enough."
~Oprah Winfrey

37

GROUP ACTION

A village working collectively accomplishes
more than any one person on their own.

The Egyptian Rekhyt is a bird called the Lapwing
which symbolizes how a group of people
working together maximizes the
shared benefits of resources and expertise.
"If we are together, nothing is impossible.
If we are divided all will fail"
~Winston Churchill

38

GROUP GOOD

A supreme priority is working
for the highest good of the group.

The Adinkra Funtunfunefu Denkyemfunefu
denotes groups of people pooling resources,
planning, and implementing...{for the} common
interest of all has a transformative effect. "...political leaders {must} be ...{honest, integrious, and
committed} to the common good...pass on to
coming generations a society of authentic justice,
solidarity, and peace." ~Pope Frances

39

HAPPINESS

Exuberance is living from
your essential self.

The Celtic symbol suggests happiness arises
from a mind which is committed to
being at peace with what is.
Gilbert Fowler White believed,
"There are only two ways to live your life.
One is as though nothing is a miracle.
The other is as though everything is a miracle."

40

HARMONY

As you go with the flow of life, the cosmos
will effortlessly support you in amazing ways.

The Cherokee symbol bespeaks consensus,
cooperation, unanimity, and understanding and
suggests honoring kinship to all of life by
maintaining balance and harmonious cooperation.
Lao Tzu reminds, "The sage is one with
the world and lives in harmony with it."

41

HARM

If you bring misfortune to any person,
place, or thing, you must make amends.

The Egyptian Chnoubis depicts
protection against disease and harm.
To what which you bring misfortune,
you must bring restitution.
"Our prime purpose in this life is
to help others. And if you can't help them,
at least don't hurt them." ~Dalai Lama XIV

42

HEALING

As you engage higher level energies, you mature and re-imprint chaotic lower level energy.

The Anasazi Spiral Sun petroglyph symbol embodies sol's consistently radiated healing power reminding us that, should the sun cease shining, there would be annihilation of everything that exists within two or three days. "Through the portals of silence the healing sun of wisdom and peace will shine upon you."
~Paramahansa Yogananda

43

IDENTIFICATION
That with which you
identify, you become.

The Phoenix Arising from the Ashes
broadcasts as a person's thoughts and
intentions evolve, all limitations can be broken.
"Sometimes you just have to die a little
inside in order to be reborn and rise again as
a stronger and wiser version of yourself."
~Aagam Shah

44

IDENTITY

You are one of a kind; no matter what,
you retain your unique fingerprint.

The Human head detailed with Fingerprint
epitomizes individual distinctiveness;
even as we merge with Source we retain
our inimitable selfhood. "Be yourself.
Everyone else is already taken."
~Oscar Wilde

45

IMPUTED KNOWLEDGE

The Source will gift you with
only as much as you can grasp.

The Tibetan Dorje represents the
attainment of enlightenment achieved by the
cutting away of ignorance and illusion.
"Where ignorance is our master, there is no
possibility of real peace."
~Dali Lama

46

INCREASE

You amplify what you focus on.

The Yantra used in Hindu and Tibetan
tantric meditation sustains a focused state;
what you dwell upon intensifies.
Focused energy is an immense power source.
"Concentrate all your thoughts upon the work
at hand. The sun's rays do not burn until
brought to a focus."
~Alexander Graham Bell

47

INFINITE EXTENSION

Ours is an infinite world of unimaginable and
never-ending learning and changes that
exist within that cosmic fire.

The Lemniscate is the symbol of infinity
and the limitless, unboundedness of the universe
around whose curves souls endlessly travel.
"The Fist law of thermodynamics tells us energy
can only be transformed; it cannot be created or
destroyed." ~Author Unknown

48

INITIATION

When you let go of the need for results,
your range of influence increases exponentially.

The Zenzar Design Initation symbol speaks to
the process of the initiatory *rite de passage*.
This process is elucidated in Goethe's *Faust* -
The Alchemical Journey.
"Faust is the spiritual seeker of truth
who undertakes the alchemical task of converting
base metal (his fallen state) into gold (his
admission to the realm of light)."

49

INNER KNOWING

All divine development is built
on living evidence of know-how.

The Blackbird bespeaks of the ability to enter the
sacred adytum, the inner holy place within
each soul that is the conduit for knowledge
between God and humanity.
"Remember, the entrance door to the
sanctuary is inside you." ~Rumi

50

INTENTION

Purpose channels the energy
needed for actualization.

The Rune Dagaz suggests resolute intention
and is suggestive of illuminative breakthroughs
and awareness. Such "white light" moments that
some call satori open you to deeply profound and
poignant comprehension. "The key to growth is
the introduction of higher dimensions of
consciousness into our awareness."
~Lao Tzu

51

INTERSTICE

From nothing comes everything.

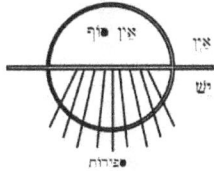

The Hebrew Ein Sof depicts how from
nothing came everything revealed and hidden.
The Source, the world, and humanity
unfold together, reflecting the desire to
perfect an imperfect world filled with
contradictions and unknowns.

52

JUDGMENT
Judge not, lest you be also judged.

The Egyptian image Assur's Beard
illustrates being judicious in speech.
"The tongue has no bones,
but is strong enough to break a heart.
So be careful with your words."
~Proverbs 15:1

53

KARMA

What you sow, so shall you reap.

The Hindu Good Karma symbol personifies
the concept of what goes around, comes around.
If the seeds of good are planted,
the return of good is harvested.
"Every moment of your life, you perform action -
physically, mentally, emotionally, and
energy-wise. Each action creates
a certain memory. That is karma."
~Sadhguru

54

KNOWLEDGE

Education provides greater wisdom to
effectively manage your life.

The Adinkra Mate Masie symbolizes
comprehension and wisdom.
Great accomplishment happens when educated,
judicious preparedness meets opportunity.
"The goal of education is the advancement of
knowledge and the dissemination of truth."
~John F. Kennedy

55

LEARNING

We learn by degrees and only after
we have focused on the lesson.

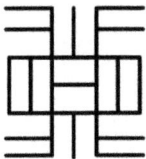

The Adinkra Nea Onnim symbolizes that
learning is limitless and takes effort and
dedication. Knowledge inspires, initiates,
and accelerates evolutionary gain on
all planes and levels of existence both
personal and universal. "Knowledge comes
from learning. Wisdom comes from living."
~Anthony Douglas Williams

56

LEAST RESISTANCE

Nature follows the principle of economy
unless redirected by a controlling agency.

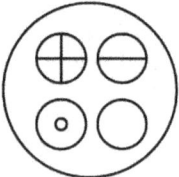

The Native American Four Elements
symbolize nature takes the path of least
resistance. The mirror effect in humankind is
to let your actions follow your conscious,
mindful heart versus bending life to your ego's
will and its illusionary choices. "Men as well as
rivers grow crooked by following the path of
least resistance." ~Thomas Jefferson

57

LIMITED EXPRESSION

All that exists is a smaller adaptation of an exponentially expanded version of itself.

The Large and Small Elephants image pays tribute to the national animal of Thailand with Buddhism as its tradition illustrating that everything is created to grow into a wiser, more evolved, version of itself. "For a man to conquer himself is the first and noblest of all victories." ~Plato

58

LOVE

Love joins.

The Heart is a universal image bespeaking love;
the Course of Miracles says, "You are asked not to
seek for love, but merely to seek and find
all the barriers within yourself
that have been built against it." When you find
within the true knowing that love and belonging,
your worth, is a birthright, that it doesn't have to
be earned, you unfold to limitless possibilities.

59

MAGIC

A shift in awareness causes
a comparable shift in the universe.

The Lesser Pentagram of Solomon symbolizes
the mysteries of theurgic, divine-driven magic.
Yes, miracles happen – both man-made
and those that remain inexplicable.
"Magic has power to experience and fathom
things which are inaccessible to human reason.
For magic is a great secret wisdom..."
~Paracelsus

60

MANIFESTATION

All things exist within the timelessness of no-time and can be called forth from the recesses of seeming emptiness.

Two Tangential Triangles connecting represents an overlay, at myriad and infinite dimensions, of connecting masculine and feminine aspects that, conjoined, give rise to creation. "If a union is to take place between opposites...it will happen in a third thing, which represents not a compromise but something new." ~Carl Jung

61

MENTALISM

Whenever you change how you look at
things, the things you look at change.

The Tamgaly, Kazakhstan, Petroglyph of
Shaman reveals they act as a conduit between the
visible world and invisible world for healing and
prophecy, shattering beliefs about what it is
possible to decree and manifest. "You simply
have to turn your back on a world...gone cold and
dead and get with the program of a living world
and the imagination." ~Terence Mckenna

62

MERCY

As you show mercy to others,
so mercy will be shown to you.

St. Catherine's Cross transmits the principle of
compassion and patience toward those
sick and suffering. Mother Theresa said,
"Although it is easier to relieve hunger with
a cup of food, it is more important to relieve
the loneliness and pain of someone unloved in
your own home for this is
where your mercy must start."

63

MYSTERY

The miracle of life is a mystery
which creates as it is created.

The Orphic Egg denotes the unnamed mystery
of chaos that created the world. Sri
Aurobindo believes, "...behind mystery is the
Consciousness lost to itself, returning to itself,
evolving out of its huge self-forgetfulness...as a
life that is would-be sentient, to be more than
sentient, to be again divinely self-conscious,
free, infinite, immortal."

64

NAMES

When you name something,
you master it.

The Ancestral Tree image legitimizes Naming
as a fundamental part of identity.
"Names have a mysterious transforming
power. ...a name may...seem accidental,
committing you to nothing, but before you
realize its magical power...it becomes part of
you and your destiny." ~Stefan Zweig

65

NEGATIVE ATTRACITON

Positive and negative
merge to create balance.

The Seal of Cagliostro shows a serpent stabbed
by an arrow representing Aleph, the union of
opposites - active and inactive, dark and light,
ego and spirit. Socrates stated if two opposite
processes did not seek to balance each other out,
there could be no change.

66

NON-COMPLETION

Nothing about existence ends; everything
evolves without needing completion.

The symbol Pi superimposed on the infinity sign
represents an ever-expansion with no point
of completion. An unknown author says,
"Pi is an infinite, non-repeating decimal. When
converted into ascii text, somewhere in that
infinite string of digits is the name of every person
you will ever love, the date, time, and manner of
your death and the answers to all the great
questions of the universe."

67

NON-INTERFERENCE

What you do not wish done to you,
do not do to another.

The Adinkra Fawohodie illumines how freedom demands living in ways that respect and reinforce the freedom of others. Einstein believed everyone acts not only under external pressure but also in compliance with inner necessity. "Never retaliate when people say unkind things about you. Pay them back with a blessing...and God will bless you." ~I Peter 3:9

68

NOW
Everything that is has always
existed and will always exist.

The Mindfulness image broadcasts the now
and contains the past, the present, and the future,
simultaneously, within the ineradicable moment.
You have the continual choice to make each moment
one of right action, right thought, and right deed.
"The ability to be in the present moment is a major
component of mental wellness."
~Abraham Maslow

69

ONE

Despite the appearance of plurality,
we are all One and in unity.

The Ringstone symbol represents humankind's interconnection to each other and ultimate connection to the Source of All. H.P. Blavatsky said, "...occult law states no man can rise superior to his individual failings without lifting the whole body of which he is an integral part. Similarly, no one can sin nor suffer its effects alone. There is no such thing as separateness."

70

PARADOX

Two seeming opposites
may both be true.

The Chinese Symbol for Koan illumines
the enigmatic nature of dualistic thinking;
intellectual reasoning by itself can't solve a
koan without breaking through lower mind
consciousness by forcing it to its limit.
"The words of truth are always paradoxical."
~Lao Tzu

71

PATTERNS

Patterns are apparent as
awareness increases.

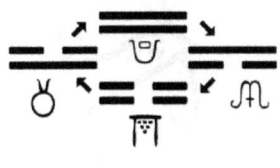

The Yin-Yang Bigrams as the Four Seasons
from the I Ching is representative of a repeating
elemental pattern; patterns are the foundation of
all levels of manifestation becoming more brilliantly
complex at higher levels of creation.
"Creativity is intelligence having fun."
~Albert Einstein

72

PEACE

Peace is always your choice no matter
what is happening outside of you.

The Reiki Shanti symbol signifies
the concept of peace which comes when
freeing yourself from ego attachments to
past hurts and future worries and by
embracing being fully present in the now.
"Peace comes from within. Do not
seek it without." ~Buddha

73

PERCEPTION

The more senses you use,
the greater your perception.

The Enneagram image is a compendium of a universal language for expanded psychological and spiritual growth leading to a true self-awakening. "Remember you come here having already understood the necessity of struggling with yourself - only with yourself. Therefore, thank everyone who gives you the opportunity." ~Gurdjieff

74

PERFECTION

Perfectionism is a mental construct;
everything is as it is supposed to be.

The Lotus symbolizes spiritual ascension, highest
enlightenment or rebirth, as a process to spiritual
perfection with the right timing of unfolding for
each soul. Sogyal Rinpoche states,
"Samsara is the mind turned outwardly, lost in
its projections. Nirvana is the mind turned
inwardly, recognizing its true nature."

75

PERMANENCE

Some souls have bodies, some do not.
Even a soul without a body continues to live.

The Medicine Man's Eye points to a higher
realization: just because something cannot be seen
does not mean it doesn't exist. "To believe in the
things you can see and touch is no belief at all;
but to believe in the unseen
is a triumph and blessing." ~Abraham Lincoln

76

PERSONAL UNIVERSE

We live in our own private worlds
rarely glimpsed by those around us.

The Labyrinth as a Papago Indian story of
emergence illustrates how others cannot totally
share all aspects of personal experience.
"Intimacy is not purely physical. It's the act
of connecting with someone so deeply you feel
like you can see into their soul."
~Author Unknown

77

POLARITY

The world operates in polarities; each part
is wholly contained within the opposite.

The Chinese Yin-Yang icon symbolizes how
opposite forces are interconnected and
interdependent and are the seed of all things.
It is a reminder that the universe and all that
is in it is both consistent and cyclical,
one force commanding and then replaced by
the opposing force in a never-ending repeat.

78

POSITIVE ATTRACTON

We are vibration energy and our energy vibrations attracts like energies.

The Maori Soul Mate symbol illustrates vibrational soul match. "We are attracted to another...at a soul level not because that person is our unique complement, but because by being with that individual, we are somehow provided with an impetus to become whole ourselves." ~Edgar Cayce

79

POTENTIALITY

That which you do not know,
or even know you have, seeks expression.

The Sufi Whirling Dervish figure represents
constant movement, capturing the motion of the
whirlies which precedes all manifestation.
"We come spinning out of nothingness, scattering
stars like dust. The stars form a circle and in
the center we dance." ~Rumi

80

PRAGMATISM

At some level, you will only do what supports
you - even if it appears contradictory.

The Chinese symbol suggests there is always a
supportive reason for any choice or action, be it
seemingly illogical or self-sabotaging. If in the
grip of self-undoing, pause. Be mindful of your
thoughts, energy, feelings, body, and spirit. Then
attend to yourself. Carl Jung says, "Until you
make the unconscious conscious, it will direct
your life and you will call it fate."

81

PROXIMITY

Whoever you identify with you will resemble.

The Greek Comedy and Tragedy Masks remind how who you surround yourself with will color your life, who you become, and how you present yourself in the world. "Surround yourself with people who make you hungry for life, touch your heart, and nourish your soul."
~Author Unknown

82

PURPOSE

Life is an expression of principles and patterns;
there is a purpose for everything.

The Shinto symbol supports life,
understanding death as a purging process
where the spirit desires to purify itself
through cycles of consciousness.
You are asked to nourish character
and right action in the physical world
in such a way that it leads to salvation
and deliverance in future incarnations.

83

RADIATION

What you are speaks so loudly it
drowns out your words.

The Zenzar Design with Bands of Energy
reflecting back and forth signifies how you
radiate feelings to others and they to you that
are more powerful than words. Live in
congruency with your beliefs, values, and
life purpose which will allow you to not only
become trustworthy but also an extraordinary
human being.

84

RECIPROCITY

Whatever you are looking for
is seeking you as well.

The Lemniscate figure Joining One Hand
Reaching for the Other implies a reality
in which what you ask for is, with the
same desire, reaching back to you.
"You are the honored guest. Do not weep
like a beggar for pieces of the world."
~Rumi

85

RECORDS

Nothing is left unrecorded;
all that ever was continues to exist.

The Open Liber Domini image with the
Egyptian Ankh announces there exists
a cinematographic record of the sum total
of all your existences. "The ancients had a
term in the mystical tradition called the
Akashic Records, which was suggestive
that nature didn't lose its experience, that the
information accumulated was available forever."
~Edgar Mitchell

86

RELEASE

What you hold onto holds onto you.

The image of Two Hands Freeing the Butterflies illustrates the concept of letting go without resentments or regrets thus freeing life to bring to you that which you would be unable to so seamlessly orchestrate on your own.

"Just remember, when you should grab something, grab it; when you should let go, let go." ~Author Unknown

87

REPETITION

Those who do not remember the lesson
repeat it with harsher consequences.

The Zenzar Design symbol of an Open Circle
moving repetitively around and around depicts
repeated re-occurrence, usually with more
intense negative consequences if the lesson
isn't learned. "The past is where you learned
the lesson; the future is where you apply it."
~Author Unknown

88

REQUEST

Love and support are as close as
your asking for them.

The image of Two Hands Reaching for
Each Other honors the spiritual truth of
how, if you ask and do not deny what is
asked for, support will be forthcoming.
"Alone we can do so little; together we can
do so much." ~Helen Keller

89

RESONANCE

Similar vibrating patterns create
similar effects in each other.

The Tibetan Holy Ohm symbol reveals
everything in existence has a frequency of
identification designed to synchronistically
function with divine guidance from the
One Source. "The original ohm, sound of all
sounds which created the universe, when intoned
vibrates the skull and the face and awakens the
light of the 3rd eye chakra." ~Author Unknown

90

SACRIFICE

Sacrifice is giving up one thing
for another of higher worth.

The Symbol of Jesus' name exemplifies how
giving up that which separates you from the
Source opens the way for greater spiritual and
psychological transformation. "The only
problem facing you in life is the belief in
separation from your Source. Solve that one
and all the other ones will vanish."
~John Randolph Price

91

SERVICE

In true service to others,
you realize yourself.

The Adinkra Boa Me Na Me Mmoa Wo
translates to "help me and I will help you."
No act of service, however small, is ever wasted.
It is by serving that we learn how to serve.
"The best way to find yourself is to lose
yourself in the service of others."
~Mahatma Gandhi

92

SHARING
Joyfully share life with others
and all will be enriched.

The image of a Pitcher of Water Pouring
suggests the power in giving. Don Marquis
writes, "There is nothing we like to see so
much as the gleam of pleasure in a person's eye
when he feels that we have sympathized with him,
understood him. At these moments something
fine and spiritual passes between two friends.
These are the moments worth living."

93

SOLAR LIGHT

The Source's governing love principle allows us
to reflect the light of our souls.

The Sun symbol represents the physical
manifestation of the Light to which all are
contracted, to which all will return, that shines
unfailingly and equally on all.
Its life-giving essence is a constant reminder
of the master plan of rebirth into a
spiritually perfected humanity.

94

SOUL CHOICE

All experiences are self-chosen for soul growth.

The symbol of a Triangle within a Circle within a Heart embodies the understanding of how the soul is aware of its foreverness. The soul sojourns to life again and again dying to old personality patterns until identification with the true and eternal "I" is achieved.

95

SOUND

A signature sound is attached to all that permeates the cosmos.

The Symbol for Ohm represents a consecrated sound preceding creation; it is a virtual compendium of sacred and mystical inspirations that communicate to your inner essence and true knowing. Ohm serves to awaken and clear the mind for meditation as well as bring about an expansion of energy and ascension.

96

SPEECH

What you say sets in motion
that which returns to you.

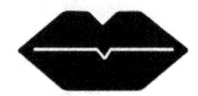

The Lip image highlights how speech influences
change and that your choice of words reveals
your level of awareness, illumination,
enlightenment, and spiritual mastery.
A Yiddish proverb says,
"A fool says what he knows
and a wise man knows what he says."

97

SURRENDER

The ego must relinquish all
in order to receive all.

The Buddha figure bespeaks of releasing all craving,
attachment, and expectation leading to the end
of the rebirth cycle and achieving Nirvana.
"...the question of Nirvana will come later. There is
not much hurry. If in day to day life you lead a
good life, with honesty, with love, with compassion,
with less selfishness, then automatically it will lead to
Nirvana." ~Dalai Lama

98

SYMBOLS

The language of all higher spheres
and beings is symbolism.

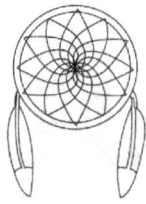

The Ojibwa Dream Catcher exemplifies how
symbols are the first language of the highest
frequencies and dimensions broadcasting
volumes of information into a very concise
space. Joseph Campbell writes that symbols
reflect spiritual or psychological principles
and powers that are timeless and
everywhere.

99

SYMMETRY

All that is naturally draws
toward greater balance.

The Pyramid symbol denotes mankind's
inner spiritual quest for unity and harmony at
ever higher vibrational planes. Necessary soul
lessons needing patience and time cannot
be avoided and must be completed for
the development of perfected humanity, which
may take many incarnations.

100

SYNCHRONICITY

You live in a synchronistic world;
coincidence is not always coincidence.

The Zenzar Design Angel Wings Surrounding
an Astrological Yod with a Hebrew Yod inside
represents purposeful coincidences, events
occurring by seeming chance that are
outside the realm of human origin.
Carl Jung believed, "Synchronicity is an ever-
present reality for those who have eyes to see."

101

SYNTHESIS

What appear to be opposites will reconcile
at a greater level of awareness.

The Ishtar Star symbol is an ancient
representation of the development of
consciousness through the spiral of space
intersected by time leading to perfect
unity encircling and embraced within plurality.
"A human being is the synthesis of the infinite
and the finite, temporal and eternal, freedom
and necessity." ~Seren Kierkegaard

102

TEACHING

The teacher and the student share equally
what is given and received.

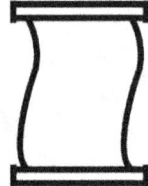

The Scroll is one of the earliest iconic
implements of the recording of information
that is passed to others through instruction
and learning. All are students and teachers
to each other in this circle of life. "A teacher
affects eternity. {S/he} can never tell when his
{or her} influence stops." ~Henry Adams

103

THOUGHT

The words you say to yourself
are who you become.

The Zenzar Design Figure of an Antenna Emitting
Waves depicts energy follows thought; what
you think you become. The daily inner work is
to relate to situations guided by universal wisdom
which allows the attainment of highest self-mastery.
"We either make ourselves miserable or we make
ourselves strong. The amount of energy
is the same" ~Carlos Castaneda

104

TRANSIENCE

Life is flux; change is not only
part of life, it is life itself.

The Volcano image depicts destruction as a
profound force which parallels the depths of
internal change possible. The ultimate goal
is to extinguish all that is untrue in the light
of Absolute Truth. "Change is the only way to
unfold all the hidden, until now, possibilities
of the 'gold in the shadow'." ~Carl Jung

105

TRANSMUTATION

One thing can change into another;
you only have to believe in the possibility.

The Philosopher's Stone is purported to contain
the knowledge of all that is, was, and will be and
represents evolution of consciousness eventuating
in the union of personal consciousness and
universal conscious in the alchemy of time.
"The elixir of life, the philosopher's stone is yours
if you surrender sterile logic, trivial reason."
~Hilda Doolittle

106

VIBRATION

All that is vibrates with
its own individual energy.

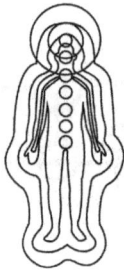

The Figure with the Energy Bodies and Chakra
Centers reflects that you are an energy being
vibrating to your current level of beliefs, emotions,
and behaviors. Your field of energy announces
you before you even speak. "If your energy body
is in full vibrancy, the physical body will
naturally fix itself." ~Sadhguru

107

VICARIOUS ATONEMENT

You always have the choice to offer yourself
in service to another's karma.

The Crown of Thorns image is an
iconic representation of Jesus taking on
humanity's karma. To take on another's karma
requires knowledge of how to take on the karma
combined with the spiritual strength to hold
that karma without being affected by it.

108

WORDS OF POWER

What you speak with purpose
determines your course.

The Siri Symbol emphasizes the power that
words exert, which can create a ripple effect
for either positive or negative consequences.
Gautama Buddha said, "Words have the power
to both destroy and heal. When words are both
true and kind, they can change the world."

Blessing

Beloved and Cherished Reader,

Always know that you are whole and complete, a singularly unique expression of Source. You are as amazing as the most luminous sunrise and as primordial as the vast firmament. You are a flame lick of divine love in human form, a spiritual being having a human experience. Through your humanity and desire for will-to-good, love's healing and lustrous, resuscitating light stream onto this planet. May you continuously tap into the source of unconditional love that is within and ever available, always reminding, "We are one." May you choose to be a conduit to the limitless, eternal mind of Source achieving its secrets, becoming one of the enlightened, caring people who will change the world raising humankind to the divine.

Themes

Balance/Harmony/Peace

- 10 - Balance
- 21 - Detachment
- 25 - Dynamic Balance
- 40 - Harmony
- 68 - Now
- 72 - Peace

Brotherhood/Planetary Cohesiveness

- 17 - Cycles
- 19 - Delegation
- 25 - Dynamic Balance
- 27 - Essence
- 37 - Group Action
- 38 - Group Good

Building Impeccable Character

- 03 - Accountability
- 14 - Consciousness
- 52 - Judgment
- 74 - Perfection
- 87 - Reputation

Co-creation

- 18 - Decree
- 19 - Delegation
- 20 - Desire

22 - Discipline
46 - Increase

Creativity/Brilliance

06 - Analogy
08 - Ascension
18 - Decree
28 - Expanded Consciousness
70 - Paradox
71 - Patterns
75 - Permanence
101 - Synchronicity
105 - Transmutation

Divine Guidance

14 - Consciousness
23 - Divine Flow
48 - Initiation
49 - Inner Knowing
63 - Mystery
89 - Resonance
95 - Sound
100 - Synchronicity

Ego Transmutation

11 - Change
14 - Consciousness
44 - Identification
50 - Intention

73 - Perception
74 - Perfection
82 - Purpose

Illumination
14 - Consciousness
28 - Expanded Consciousness
45 - Imputed Knowledge
47 - Infinite Extension
78 - Positive Attraction
94 - Soul Choice

Intuitional Guidance
23 - Divine Flow
28 - Expanded Consciousness
45 - Imputed Knowledge
49 - Inner Knowing
63 - Mystery

Integrity
69 - One
84 - Reciprocity
87 - Reputation
102 - Synthesis
108 - Words of Power

Karmic Redemption
10 - Balance
41 - Harm

- 53 - Karma
- 85 - Records
- 87 - Repetition
- 95 - Soul Choice
- 107 - Vicarious Atonement

Liberation From the Cycles of Birth and Death
- 41 - Harm
- 67 - Non-Interference
- 74 - Perfection
- 85 - Records
- 95 - Soul Choice
- 97 - Surrender
- 105 - Transcience

Loving Response to Life
- 12 - Compassion
- 34 - Goodwill
- 58 - Love
- 62 - Mercy
- 69 - One

Manifesting
- 01 - Abundance
- 18 - Decree
- 23 - Divine Flow
- 46 - Increase
- 60 - Manifestation
- 77 - Polarity

78 - Positive Attraction
79 - Potentiality

Mindfulness

08 - Ascension
16 - Continuity of Consciousness
21 - Detachment
24 - Divine Oneness
27 - Essence
96 - Speech

Perfected Humanity

11 - Change
22 - Discipline
24 - Divine Oneness
25 - Dynamic Balance
69 - One
92 - Service
99 - Symmetry

Self-Mastery

56 - Least Resistance
72 - Peace
75 - Permanence
82 - Purpose
103 - Thought
108 - Words of Power

Self-Realization
- 45 - Imputed Knowledge
- 76 - Personal Universe
- 83 - Radiation
- 102 - Teaching

Service to Humanity
- 24 - Divine Oneness
- 28 - Expanded Consciousness
- 29 - Essence
- 62 - Mercy
- 90 - Sacrifice
- 91 - Service
- 92 - Sharing

Shamanism
- 45 - Imputed Knowledge
- 59 - Magic
- 61 - Mentalism
- 99 - Symbols
- 105 - Transcience

Spiritual Awakening and Deepening
- 05 - Akasha
- 07 - As Above, So Below
- 28 - Expanded Knowledge
- 91 - Sacrifice
- 106 - Vibration

Stress Reduction
- 02 - Acceptance
- 10 - Balance
- 23 - Divine Flow
- 67 - Non-Interference
- 98 - Surrender

Transmuted Consciousness
- 23 - Divine Flow
- 83 - Radiation
- 84 - Reciprocity
- 104 - Thought
- 105 - Transmutation

Transmutation of the World Soul
- 42 - Healing
- 91 - Sacrifice
- 92 - Service
- 94 - Solar Light
- 107 - Vicarious Atonement

Virtuousness
- 12 - Compassion
- 30 - Forgiveness
- 33 - Giving
- 34 - Goodwill
- 35 - Grace
- 57 - Love
- 62 - Mercy

Contributors

Barbara Davis-Thompson, LCSW is a psychotherapist in private practice in New York City. She has her MSW from Fordham University and a MA from New York University. She is an eternal student continuing to learn new modalities of therapy and undertaking new spiritual pathways to truth.

Her professional trainings have been in Freudian and Jungian Psychology, EMDR, Heart-Centered Hypnotherapy, Brain-spotting, AEDP, Sensorimotor Therapy, Coherence Therapy, Biofeedback, EFT for couples, Addictions and Ro-Hun. She continues to study with BOTA, Ltd. Recently she has incorporated into her work the Lucia Light Experience. She lives in NYC with her husband Mike and is the loving mother of Christopher, Barrett, and daughter-in-law Mischelle Weedman-Davis and the proud grandmother of Hannah McKenna and Jackson Boone.

Joshua J. Mark is a part-time professor at Marist College and editor/writer for Ancient History Encyclopedia. He has travelled and studied in Egypt and lived in Greece and Germany.

His work with ancient history, especially Egyptian and Mesopotamian history, often involves interpretation and identification of symbols and the patterns of culture and spirituality symbols express. Mark is also staff writer for Timeless Travels Magazine and a freelance contributor to magazines such as History Ireland and Ancient Warfare. He lives in upstate New York with his wife, Betsy, and daughter Emily.

Special Acknowledgements

Gail Baral, business strategy coach, for her guidance and support in creating Zenzar Design, LLC, designing the Symbol Lamp, and editing *Symbol Odyssey: Guidebook to the 108 Uncompromising Principles of Wisdom and Truth.*

Mischelle Weedman-Davis, for her time and support in the creation of the Symbol Lamp and *Symbol Odyssey: Guidebook to the 108 Uncompromising Principles of Wisdom and Truth.*

Kevin Yong-Moon Lee, artist, visionary and musician, for executing the vision of the Symbol Lamp and for his innumerable help in formatting *Symbol Odyssey: Guidebook to the 108 Uncompromising Principles of Wisdom and Truth.*

Robin Pelkki, RN and former Creative Director at Book of the Month Club, for her typographical thoughts on formatting: *Symbol Odyssey: Guidebook to the 108 Uncompromising Principles of Wisdom and Truth.*

Twoworldswisdom.org, for acknowledging the universal truths are free use to humanity.

Resources

Abu'l-Baha: QuoteFancy.com - "The most important principle of divine philosophy is the oneness..."

Henry Adams: https://en.wikiquote.org/wiki/Henry_Adams - "A teacher affects..."

Isabel Allende: AZQuotes - "We only have what we..."

Debbie Zylstra Almstedt: Zibu: The Power of Angelic Symbology

Marcus Aurelius: Meditations

Sri Aurobindo: azquotes.com - "But what after all, behind appearance is the..."

Author Unknown: afuntanilla.wordpress.com/favorite-quotes/ - "A comfort zone is a beautiful..."

Author Unknown: Goodmath/Badmath.com - "Pi is an infinite, non-repeating decimal..."

Author Unknown: www.healingsounds.com/planetary-healing-sounds/ - "The original ohm, the sound of..."

Author Unknown: www.pinterest.com/pin/88735055132608832/ - "Accept what is..."

Author Unknown://www.pinterest.com/pin/301670875013897892/ - "Friendship is not about..."

Author Unknown://www.pinterest.com/pin/56083957834810311/ - "Surround yourself..."

Author Unknown: Pinterest.com - "Your largest fear carries your greatest..."

Author Unknown: Pinterest.com - "Imagine how the..."

Author Unknown: https://www.pinterest.com/pin/130393351684666907/ - "Intimacy is not..."

Author Unknown: https://au.pinterest.com/pin/459789443185855926/ - "Reincarnation is in..."

Author Unknown: yousephtanha.com/blog/2008/05/.../ "do-the-things-you-own-end..."

Marcus Aurelius: Meditations

Sarah Bartlett: The Secrets of the Universe in 100 Symbols

Sun Bear, Wabun Wind and Chrysalis Mulligan: Dancing with the Wheel: The Medicine Wheel Workbook

Alexander Graham Bell: QuotesValley.com - "Concentrate all your thoughts..."

Charles Benn: China's Golden Age: Everyday Life in the Tang Dynasty

The Bible: I Peter 3:9: https://pinterest.com - "Never retaliate when people say unkind..."

The Bible: Proverbs 15:1: www.pinterest.com/pin/37830243 7429355568/ - "The tongue has no bones..."

Hans Biedermann: Dictionary of Symbolism: Cultural Icons and the Meanings Behind Them

H. P. Blavatsky: www.awaken.com/2013/05/quotes-by-madame-blavatsky/ - "...occult law states no man can rise..."

Ralph H. Blum: The Book of Runes

D. Bostock: Plato's Phaedo

Miranda Bruce-Mitford: Signs & Symbols: An Illustrated Guide to Their Origins and Meanings

Buddha: thinkexist.com/.../peace_comes_from_within-do_not_seek_it_without/147331.html

Buddha: www.wordresults.com/blog.html - "Words have the power to both..."

Builders of the Adytum: The Hebrew Letters, A Workbook

Kathy L. Callahan: The Path of the Medicine Wheel: A Guide to the Sacred Circle

Julia Cameron: The Artist's Way: A Spiritual Path to Higher Creativity

Joseph Campbell: https://www.quotemaster.org qc49daed154517853415b6037e057ba46 "...symbols...refer..."

Paul Case: Builders of the Adytum, Ltd. - Mystery School in the Western Tradition

Carlos Castaneda: pinterest.com/pin/483574078713124427/ - "We either make ourselves..."

Edgar Cayce: https: books.google.com/books?isbn=1944068473 - "We are attracted..."

Pema Chodron: www.facebook.com/Pema.Chodron/posts/10153746616258220 - "...karma...continually..."

Winston Churchill: azquotes - "If we are together..."

Jean Dalby Clift and Wallace B. Clift: Symbols of Transformation in Dreams

Paulo Coelho: https://www.facebook.com/paulocoelho/posts/10150294688951211 - "When you say "yes"..."

Course of Miracles: https://www.facim.org/online-learning-aids/.../a-course-in-miracles-a.../part-xii.aspx - "You are..."

David N. Daniels and Virginia A. Price: The Essential Enneagram: The Definitive Personality Test and Self-Discovery Guide

Hilda Doolittle: azquotes - "The elixir..."

Wayne Dyer: The Essential Wayne Dyer Collection

Albert Einstein: www.values.com/inspirational-quotes/7486-creativity-is-intelligence-having-fun

Black Elk: www.goodreads.com/quotes/542709-i-did-not-see-anything..."

Epictetus: Enchiridion

Pope Frances: azquotes.com - "It is..necessary...that political leaders be ..."

Benjamin Franklin: QuoteFancy.com - "Never ruin an apology..."

Mahatma Ghandi: https://www.brainyquote.com/quotes/quotes/m/mahatmagan120119.html - "Action expresses..."

Mahatma Ghandi: www.thequotes.in - "If the courage to endure..."

Mahatma Ghandi: https://www.enotes.com › Homework Help› Mahatma Gandhi - "The best way to..."

William G. Gray: Cabalistic Concepts: Living the Tree

Stanislav Grof: izquotes.com/quote/76319 - "In the kind of world we have today, transformation of humanity..."

G. I. Gurdjief: www.goodreads.com/.../658571-"remember-you-come-..."

Richard P. Hayes: Land of No Buddha: Reflections of a Sceptical Buddhist

Napoleon Hill: www.brainyquote.com/quotes/quotes/n/napoleonhi165555.html - "Desire is the starting..."

Robert E. Hinshaw: Living with Nature's Extremes: The Life of Gilbert Fowler White

Mark Hosak and Walter Lubbock: The Big Book of Reiki Symbols: The Spiritual Transition of Symbols and Mantras of the Usui System of Natural Healing

Thomas Jefferson: quotemaster.org/ qb3279a3eab6f316296ab1f47ec4b2285 - "Men as well as..."

Carl Jung: https://www.elephantjournal.com/2014/.../synchronicity-for-those-who-have-eyes-to...

Carl Jung: Goethe's Faust - The Alchemical Journey. "Faust is the spiritual..."

Carl Jung: https://www.pinterest.com/explore/carl-jung-quotes/ - "Change is the only way..."

Carl Jung: https://www.pinterest.com/explore/carl-jung-quotes/ - "If a union is to take place between..."

John F. Kennedy: forum.thefreedictionary.com - "The goal of education is the advancement of..."

Seren Kierkegaard: statusmind.com/clever-facebook-status-2630/ - "A human..."

Rudolf Koch: The Book of Signs

John M. Koller: Asian Philosophies

Isidore Kozminsky: Zodiacal Symbology and its Planetary Power

Paul Kriwaczek: Babylon: Mesopotamia and the Birth of Civilization

Dalai Lama: nibbanaspace.blogspot.sg/2011/12/nirvana.html?m=1 - "There is not much hurry..."

Dalai Lama: QuoteHD.com - "Where ignorance is your master, there is no possibility of..."

Dalai Lama: QuoteFancy.com - "Our prime..."

Dalai Lama: QuotePixel.com - "Love and..."

Anne Lamott: Pinterest.com - "I do not at all ..."

Blessed Lanfranc: The Past Life of Swami Sri Yukteswar, Guru of Paramahansa Yogananda

C.W. Leadbeater: Ancient Mystic Rites

C.S. Lewis: The Discarded Image: An Introduction to Medieval and Renaissance Literature

Abraham Lincoln: https://books.google.com/books?isbn=1482851326 - "To believe..."

Chief Arvol Looking Horse: Pinterest.com - "Everything has a spirit...."

Terence McKenna: www.goodreads.com/.../7391624- "we-have-gone-sick-by-following-a-path-of-..."

Tau Malachi: Gnosis of the Cosmic Christ: A Gnostic Christian Kabbalah

Don Marquis: quotepixel.com/.../don_marquis - "There is nothing..."

Abraham Maslow: izquotes.com - "The ability to be in the present..."

Margaret Mead: www.bluestockingclub.org/bluestocking-club-history.html - "Never believe..."

James B. Miles: The Free Will Delusion: How We Settled for the Illusion of Morality

Edgar Mitchell: www.azquotes.com - "The ancients..."

Adele Nozedar: Illustrated Signs & Symbols Sourcebook - An A to Z Compendium of over 1000 Designs

Paracelsus: https://books.google.com/books?isbn=064643327X - "Magic has power to ..."

Plato: https://www.pinterest.com/pin/317714948682915242 - "For a man to conquer..."

John Randolph Price: azquotes.com - "The only problem facing you ..."

Psalms 82:6: www.godlikeproductions.com/forum1/message3509985/pg1 - "Ye are gods..."

David Reichenstein: Die Religion der Gebildeten Lati

Rinpoche: Death, Intermediate State, and Rebirth

Richard Rohr: Falling Upward: A Spirituality for the Two Halves of Life

W.H.D. Rouse: Great Dialogues of Plato [Complete Texts of The Republic, Apology, Crito, Phaedo, Ion, Meno, Symposium]

Rumi: www.goodreads.com/.../643821-i-searched-for-god-and-found-only-myself-i-searched..."

Rumi: https://www.pinterest.com/pin/547398529693375944/ - "We come in out of nothingness, scattering stars..."

Rumi: https://www.pinterest.com/pin/259731103480385917/ - "You are the honored..."

Rumi: https://theoldproverbialrecovery.wordpress.com/.../ "remember-the-entrance-door-to-the..."

Ward Rutherford: Celtic Lore - The History of the Druids and Their Timeless Traditions

Sadhguru: https://www.pinterest.com/pin/330029478918287873/ - "If your energy..."

Sadhguru: wisespiritualideas.blogspot.com/2014/08/great-quotes-from-sadhguru-jaggi.html - "Every moment of your life you perform action..."

Saint Juan de la Cruz: "Ascent of Mount Carmel"

Saint Juan de la Cruz: "Dark Night of the Soul"

Jamie Sams: Dancing the Dream: The Seven Sacred Paths of Human Transformation

Albert Schweitzer: https://libquotes.com/albert-schweitzer/quote/lby7q9p - "All art speaks in signs..."

Albert Schweitzer: quoteaddicts.com/topic/ethics- quotes-from-great-philosophers/ - "Man's ethics must..."

Helen Schucman and William Thetford: A Course in Miracles

Chief Seattle: californiaindianeducation.org/famous_indian_ chiefs/chief_seattle/ -"Humankind has not..."

Agar Shah: www.goodreads.com/quotes/7623492- "sometimes-you-just-have-to-die-a-little-inside-in..."

Michael A. Singer: The Untethered Soul: The Journey Beyond Yourself

Sogyal Rinpoche: www.awakening-intuition.com/samsara-quotes.html - "Samsara is the mind..."

Stephen F. Teiser: Reinventing the Wheel: Paintings of Rebirth in Medieval Buddhist Temples

Nikola Tesla: QuotesAddicts.com - "My brain is ..."

Mother Theresa: www.goodngreat.com - "It's not how much we give, but how much love we put..."

Mother Theresa: https://www.pinterest.com/explore/ mother-teresa/ - "Although it is easier to relieve..."

Eckhart Tolle: The Power of Now

Leo Tolstoy: www.quotationspage.com/quote/4147.html - "Truth, like gold..."

Hermes Trismegistus: doglover.pw/tags/asabovesobelow - "The universe is the same as..."

Ludvig von Beethoven: https://www.reddit.com/r/ - request "Don't only practice your art but..."

Johann Wolfgang von Goethe: izquotes.com - "So divinely is our world organized that..."

Edward Waite and Pamela Colman Smith: The Rider Tarot Deck

Brian L. Weiss: Many Lives, Many Masters

Oscar Wilde: Lookupquotes.com - "Be yourself; everyone else is..."

Anthony Douglas Williams: www.aaanything.net/.../knowledge-comes-from-learning-wisdom-comes..."

Oprah Winfrey: izquotes.com - "Be thankful for what you have; you'll ..."

Yiddish Proverb: https://www.pinterest.com/pin/394768723556277479/ - "A fool says what..."

Paramahansa Yogananda: azquotes.com - "Through the portals of silence the healing..."

Paramahansa Yogananda: 9dailyquotes.com - "The Creator, in taking infinite pains..."

Stefan Zweig: azquotes.com - "Names have a mysterious transforming..."

www.ingramcontent.com/pod-product-compliance
Lightning Source LLC
Chambersburg PA
CBHW071513040426
42444CB00008B/1626